Flowing

In The Anointing

By

Jack Myers

Jack Myers Ministries
World Revival Evangelistic Association, Inc.
Broken Arrow, Oklahoma
www.JackMyersMinistries.com
Jmm.Revival@juno.com

ISBN: 0-9720928-1-1

Published by Jack Myers Ministries World Revival
Evangelistic Association, Inc.

Jack Myers Ministries Publishing Department
Broken Arrow, Oklahoma
Editing by Becky Hurlstone

Book cover & text design by Jack Myers Ministries, Inc.
All rights reserved.

Dedication

I dedicate this book to my lovely wife Marie and my two wonderful sons John and Joshua; thank you for all your patience and understanding. To all of our friends and partners in this ministry who helped complete this work, I am eternally thankful.

The Anointing: Nothing Less - Nothing More.

Evangelist Jack Myers

Contents

Introduction

Over many years of ministering to God's people, I have shared the message of the anointing in churches with as few as five members and with as many as five thousand members. I have witnessed thousands of people coming to the altar to give or rededicate their hearts to God when the anointing falls in a service. I have seen the power of God set people free from smoking, deliver from demons, and heal people of many ailments. Two things have done it all. One: the name of Jesus; Two: the power of the anointing.

My prayer for you is that you understand and experience the power of the anointing. I believe in the pages of this book you will discover the truths of God's word pertaining to the anointing. I believe whether you are in the full time ministry or just a believer in Jesus, you will discover how to operate in the anointing of God.

I have taught in denominational and non-denominational churches throughout the United States and in several other nations. I have discovered in my travels that most people are hungry for the anointing of God and desire to operate in His power. I believe you will be blessed by this book and have a better understanding of what the anointing is and how you can begin your journey to *Flowing In The Anointing.*

Chapter One
What Is The Anointing?

As I was ministering in a church in the country of Honduras, I called for those that wanted a touch from heaven. The people began to gather up near the front of the platform. There were about sixty people that came close to the platform. I asked them to lift their hands. As they lifted their hands toward heaven, I shouted, "Be filled with the Holy Spirit in Jesus' name!" As I said this, the power of the anointing came down from heaven and all sixty fell to the floor.

What an awesome display of God's anointing I saw that day!

Without the anointing of God, it is impossible to flow in the supernatural power of God. Understanding the working principles of the anointing will enable us to live victoriously in the Lord ourselves and increase our ability to minister to others.

To better understand the anointing, we will begin with a few definitions. Webster's Dictionary says that the anointing is "the act of smearing with oil; a consecrating."

Strong's Exhaustive Concordance gives the definition as follows: "An unguent or smearing, i.e. (figuratively) the special endowment (chrism) of the Holy Spirit: anointing, or unction."

Vine's Expository Dictionary (under "Charisma") makes it clear: "That believers have 'an anointing from the Holy One' indicates that this anointing renders them holy, separating them to God."

We can conclude that God is the source of the anointing, and that He separates us from the world for His purposes; and that He paints, smears, and rubs His ability on us, so that we will bring glory and honor to Him. The anointing is God's supernatural ability and it is far above any human ability.

The Anointing Should Not Be Confused With Talent

A talented person is able to function easily in some areas that others find a real struggle. Talent can influence, inspire and persuade others to a limited degree but only God's anointing is unlimited in what it accomplishes!

For example: Just because someone can sing like a mocking bird does not mean they are operating by the anointing. You can see this in the church as well as in the world. Just because a person can teach or preach or orate does not mean that he or she is operating by the anointing.

If a person leans more on his own ability than on God's ability, when it comes time for him to minister the yoke-destroying power of God to others, there is no manifested presence of God: his ability overrides God's ability and there is no anointing. We then run short of what God desires, which is for every person to walk in the power of the anointing. There are people that God has anointed with His ability and they can preach, teach, or sing by His power and in addition, bound people receive their liberty because God's manifested presence destroys their yokes of bondage. We read in Acts 10:38: "How God anointed Jesus of Nazareth with the Holy Ghost and with power: who went about doing good and healing all who were oppressed of the devil; for God was with Him." Jesus could not operate in the anointing until the Holy Spirit anointed Him.

When Did Jesus Become Anointed?

Jesus became anointed when John baptized him in Luke chapter three (see Luke 3:21-23). After Jesus became anointed, His first miracle was when He turned water into wine at the wedding feast in Cana of Galilee.

Since God has conformed us to the image of "Christ"- The Anointed - Jesus, we can also be anointed to do good and to heal all that are oppressed of the devil (See Romans 8:29 and John14:12 and Luke 4:18). It is all done by the name of Jesus and the power of the anointing.

God's manifested presence is the anointing that can destroy the yokes of bondage in a person's life. People can be bound in many areas: in their physical bodies by sickness and disease; strongholds in their minds; in their emotions; in their circumstances; by poverty and lack; by fear, doubt and unbelief; the list goes on and on, but the anointing can destroy all these bondages. "And it shall come to pass in that day, [that] his burden shall be taken away from off thy shoulder, and his yoke from off thy neck, and the yoke shall be destroyed because of the anointing." (Isaiah 10:27)

The Invisible Substance

The anointing is the invisible substance that abides in us

8

and is released through us to bring deliverance to those that are held captive by the devil (see I Corinthians 4:18). Keep on reading, I will get to what that substance is.

Many times when I preach on the anointing, God will have me demonstrate. I remember being in a church in Cherryvale, Ks. It was a Pentecostal Holiness Church. At that time in our ministry we had a praise and worship leader who traveled part of the time with my family. This particular time, our praise and worship leader came with us. As I got to the point in my message about how the anointing is transferable, I asked our worship leader to stand. As she did, I said to her, "When I hand you my Bible and say, 'In the name of Jesus', the power of God will go right through you."

"You just receive it, Ok!" She said, "Ok!"

As I handed her my Bible and said, "In the name of Jesus," she was thrown to the floor like lightning; she was not hurt, just overcome by God's power. I explained to the congregation that the word of God is powerful and just as anointed as Jesus Himself is. Why is that? That is because *Jesus is the Word.* Jesus also openly demonstrated to a crowd in the book of Mark chapter 3:3-5; this portion of scripture relates to the man with the withered hand.

Jesus was ministering to a crowd and asked a man to stand in front of everyone and stretch forth his withered hand. As the man obeyed Jesus, his hand was restored to perfection. What caused this man's hand to be healed? It was the anointing of God.

The Ability To Witness

When the anointing of God is flowing through us, we become bold witnesses for Jesus. The anointing helps us witness in two ways. One: Through the sharing of our faith with others and Two: In the demonstration of the power of God through us. "But ye shall receive power, after that the Holy Ghost is come upon you: and ye shall be witnesses unto me both in Jerusalem, and in all Judea, and in Samaria, and unto the uttermost part of the earth." (Acts 1:8)

Earlier we mentioned the difference between talent and the anointing. The apostle Paul was dependent upon the anointing to accomplish God's purposes in his ministry and he used God's ability and not his own. In I Corinthians 2:5-6, he expressed this truth: "And my speech and my preaching was not with enticing words of man's wisdom, *but in demonstration of the Spirit and of power:* that your faith should not stand in the wisdom of men, but in the power of God." (italics mine)

What could be a more awesome way to be a witness for the Lord Jesus than to be able to display His Glory and Power in the Church and in the world!

Examples In The Natural World

The anointing of God is an invisible substance that can produce visible effects. One example of this in the natural world would be the wind. We cannot see the wind itself with our physical eyes, but we can certainly see some of the results of its action. When a gale force wind moves across a land mass, it can even change the appearance of the landscape by blowing down trees and destroying buildings. Another example of the anointing in the natural would be electricity. Electricity is one of the most powerful resources found on our planet; it is also one of the most useful. Harnessed properly, this one source of power can accomplish a number of things. The same power that keeps the light bulbs lit can also run the air conditioner. Inside the walls of buildings, we find conduits containing electrical wires.

These wires are the conductive material through which the electricity flows. If any of these wires were exposed and you touched one of these 'live wires', you would feel a surge of electrical power. It would be a shocking experience for you. If the voltage was great enough, it would kill you. But, believe me, even a small amount of electricity makes a lasting impression! If you don't believe me, you could go to an electrical outlet and stick your finger in it to see what will happen - but I would not recommend it. Let me share with you a different type of shocking experience.

A Shocking Experience

About 9 years ago, I was asked to minister in a chapel service for a private high school in Tampa, Florida. I began to minister to the youth about the Lord Jesus and His great delivering power. The young people seemed to be very alert and on the edges of their seats.

When it came time for the altar call, many of the young people came forward to either give their hearts to the Lord or to rededicate themselves to Him. After I led them in a short prayer of salvation and rededication, I began to lay my hand on each one of them and ask the Lord to bless them.

As I went down the line of students praying for them

through the laying on of hands, a few of them fell to the floor as if some unseen force had hit them. After the service, one young lady shared that she had never experienced that kind of touch from God before. She said that when I placed my hand on her head she felt something like electricity that went right through her. It really startled her, and a reality of God's presence came into her life.

The anointing became a tangible substance that this young lady experienced. The anointing made an impact and an impression in her life. Many times people have told me that they have seen a flash of light when I laid my hands on them, or they felt like electricity went through them.

When the anointing comes in contact with human flesh, a lasting change will take place. In the Old Testament, we see that oil mixed with specific spices was used to anoint the priests and all the articles used in the temple for worship. This signified that whatever was anointed was separated unto God and is set aside for His purposes.

Even so, today the anointing of God is what is needed to separate us from any other religion in the world and proves that Jesus did come in the flesh and that He is alive today, and that He is still doing signs and wonders today.

The Convincing Factor

When I went to the country of Nepal, I found that one of the things that convinces Buddhists and Hindus that Jesus is the living God are the miracles they receive. You see, Buddhists and Hindus serve thirty-three million male and female gods. Buddhists and Hindus do not have a problem receiving Jesus as another god. But the convincing factor that helps them in putting aside all their other gods and making Jesus the only true God is when they experience the anointing of God's power that saves, heals, and delivers them from the bondages of the devil.

The anointing is the manifested presence of God and we must learn to know and flow with His presence. We must learn to flow with and discover what the anointing is and when and how to operate in it. For it is in His anointing and presence every person's needs will be supplied. "But my God shall supply all your need according to his riches in glory by Christ [the anointed or anointing] Jesus."
(Phil 4:19 paraphrase mine)

Descriptions Of The Anointing

In the Word of God, there are several different descriptions of the anointing. Here is a list of some of them and the scripture references where they are found.

The Hand of the Lord
Ezekiel 1:3 "The word of the LORD came expressly unto Ezekiel the priest, the son of Buzi, in the land of the Chaldeans by the river Chebar; and the hand of the LORD was there upon him."

Oil
Exodus 29:7 "Then shalt thou take the anointing oil, and Pour [it] upon his head, and anoint him."

Rain
Zec 10:1 "Ask ye of the LORD rain in the time of the latter rain; [so] the LORD shall make bright clouds, and give them showers of rain, to every one grass in the field."

Cloud

2 Chr 5:13 "It came even to pass, as the trumpeters and singers [were] as one, to make one sound to be heard in praising and thanking the LORD; and when they lifted up [their] voice with the trumpets and cymbals and instruments of music, and praised the LORD, [saying], For [he is] good; for his mercy [endureth] for ever: that [then] the house was filled with a cloud, [even] the house of the LORD."

Glory

Exodus 24:16 "And the glory of the LORD abode upon mount Sinai, and the cloud covered it six days: and the seventh day he called unto Moses out of the midst of the cloud."

Dew

Psalm 133:3 "As the dew of Hermon, [and as the dew] that descended upon the mountains of Zion: for there the LORD commanded the blessing, [even] life for evermore."

Water

Isa 44:3 "For I will pour water upon him that is thirsty, and floods upon the dry ground: I will pour my spirit upon thy seed, and my blessing upon thine offspring."

River

John 7:38 "He that believeth on me, as the scripture hath said, out of his belly shall flow rivers of living water."

Wind

John 3:8 "The wind bloweth where it listeth, and thou hearest the sound thereof, but canst not tell whence it cometh, and whither it goeth: so is every one that is born of the Spirit."

Fire

1 Kings 18:38 "Then the fire of the LORD fell, and consumed the burnt sacrifice, and the wood, and the stones, and the dust, and licked up the water that [was] in the trench."

Unction

1 John 2:20 "But ye have an unction from the Holy One, and ye know all things."

Spirit

John 1:32 "And John bare record, saying, I saw the Spirit descending from heaven like a dove, and it abode upon him."

Power

Acts 1:8 "But ye shall receive power, after that the Holy Ghost is come upon you: and ye shall be witnesses unto me both in Jerusalem, and in all Judea, and in Samaria, and unto the uttermost part of the earth."

Once you understand that the anointing is the power side of God and that it is the substance of the manifested presence of God in the natural and that the anointing is what we need to get results for the kingdom of God, we can move on to explain the role of the Holy Spirit.

Chapter Two

The Role Of The Holy Spirit

Another aspect in understanding the anointing of God is the role of the Holy Spirit. First we must establish the fact that the Holy Spirit is a person: He is not a dove; He is not an "It"; He is the third person of the Godhead. God the Father, God the Son, and God the Holy Spirit. They are three, but one. It is difficult to explain the Trinity but the word of God is clear.

The Godhead is three, but they are also one. An example that might help is this: I am one person, yet I am known as a son, as a husband, as a dad, as a friend, an evangelist, etc. I display different characteristics in the different roles. But I am one being with different aspects. Another example is water. Water can be liquid, or vapor, or ice, but it is still water.

"For there are three that bear record in heaven, the Father (*God*), the Word (*Jesus*), and the Holy Ghost (*The Spirit*): and these three are one. And there are three that bear witness in earth, the Spirit (*God*), and the Water (*Holy Ghost*), and the blood (*Jesus*): and these three agree in one."
(1 John 5:7, 8 paraphrase and italics mine)

The Holy Spirit, also known as the Holy Ghost, is the power side of God. He was involved in the beginning at the creation of the world. "And the earth was without form, and void; and darkness [was] upon the face of the deep. And the *Spirit of God* moved upon the face of the waters." (Genesis 1:2 italics mine)

It was also the power of the Holy Spirit that raised Jesus from the dead. "But if the Spirit of him that raised up Jesus from the dead dwell in you, he that raised up Christ from the dead shall also quicken your mortal bodies by his Spirit that dwelleth in you." (Romans 8:11)

The Holy Spirit's power has not diminished and He is actively involved in our lives today. It is vital to understand that when a person receives Jesus as Lord and Savior that he receives the Father, the Son, and the Holy Spirit. No one member of the Godhead is less important than the others. But the Holy Spirit has a unique role in every believer's life.

The Greek word "paraclete" shows us that the Holy Spirit is the one who is called alongside to help us. He is our helper, counselor, advocate, comforter, strengthener, teacher, intercessor, and friend. (see John 14:26, AMP)

He knows what is in the mind of God and His perfect will for our lives. The Holy Spirit never draws attention to Himself, He always draws attention to Jesus and glorifies Him. The Holy Spirit took the place of Jesus on the earth.

We as believers need to get to know the Holy Spirit, who He is, and what He does.

Spending Time With The Holy Spirit

Just as the best way to become better acquainted with a person in the natural is to spend time with him or her, the same principle applies to our relationship with the Holy Spirit. Remember, He is a person. You may ask how we can spend time with someone that we cannot see.

Anything and everything we do in our relationship with God is done by faith.

Faith simply believes that something is real even before we have the natural evidence of touch, sight, or feeling to prove it. We operate in principles of faith every day. If you've ever sat in a chair without being concerned that it would collapse beneath you or turned a light on by flipping the switch, you have operated in faith.

In order to know the Holy Spirit better, we must commune with Him. Spending time with the Holy Spirit consists of talking with Him, worshipping Him and inviting Him to come and be with you. Ask Him to teach and reveal God's word to you. Praying and singing in the Holy Spirit plays a very important part in the process of building a relationship with Him: this helps your spirit get in tune with the Holy Spirit. He enables us to pray in the Spirit after we have been baptized into Him.

What I mean by this is that we are given a heavenly prayer language.

"And, being assembled together with [them], commanded them that they should not depart from Jerusalem, but wait for the promise of the Father, which, [saith he], ye have heard of me. For John truly baptized with water; but ye shall be baptized with the Holy Ghost not many days hence." (Acts 1:4-5)

"And they were all filled or (Baptized) with the Holy Ghost, and began to speak with other tongues, as the Spirit gave them utterance." (Acts 2:4, paraphrase mine) We will go into more detail about the importance of praying in the Spirit later in this chapter.

The Fruit Of The Spirit

When a Believer allows the Holy Spirit to be a dominant factor in his life, there will be an evidence of that and it will be clearly seen. A person will begin to show the same attitudes and attributes that the Holy Spirit does. When I asked the Lord what distinguishes a mature Christian from an immature Christian, He showed me that a person who dictates his life by the fruit of the Spirit is one who is mature in the faith.

A carnal Christian is a person who dictates his life by the flesh or his selfish nature. For example, take two born again Christians: one has only been born again for one year and the other for twenty years. The one that has been born again for one year can be more mature spiritually than the one that has been born again for twenty years. This will occur if the one that has been born again for one year is dictating his life by the Holy Spirit within him while the one that has been born again twenty years is dictating his life by his circumstances and his carnal selfish desires.

Maturity is not determined by the length of time that one has known the Lord, but by what dominates his or her life.

Galatians chapter 5 shows the works of the flesh in contrast with the fruit of the Spirit. "Now the works of the flesh are manifest, which are [these]; adultery, fornication, uncleanness, lasciviousness, Idolatry, witchcraft, hatred, variance, emulations, wrath, strife, seditions, heresies, envyings, murders, drunkenness, revellings, and such like: of the which I tell you before, as I have also told [you] in time past, that they which do such things shall not inherit the kingdom of God. But the fruit of the Spirit is love, joy, peace, longsuffering, gentleness, goodness, faith, Meekness, temperance: against such there is no law." (Galatians 5:19-23)

Grieving & Quenching The Holy Spirit

Like any other person, the Holy Spirit has feelings and can be grieved. How does one grieve the Holy Spirit? The word "grieve" means to cause sorrow. When does a person cause sorrow to the Holy Spirit? Our attitudes, words, and actions can all cause grief. In Ephesians chapter four we see that how we behave in our relationships with others can greatly affect the Holy Spirit.

"And grieve not the Holy Spirit of God, whereby ye are sealed unto the day of redemption. Let all bitterness, and wrath, and anger, and clamor, and evil speaking, be put away from you, with all malice: And be ye kind one to another, tenderhearted, forgiving one another, even as God for Christ's sake hath forgiven you." (Ephesians 4:30-32)

If we as believers do not forgive each other and treat one another kindly and speak about each other as Jesus would, we grieve the Holy Spirit.

How Does An Individual Quench The Holy Spirit?

Some seem to believe that the Holy Spirit is quenched when a sound system in a church goes haywire or when ushers are directing people in a prayer line; or possibly when a baby is crying loudly in a service. Yes, these things can distract us, but these things do not quench or grieve the Holy Spirit or distract Him.

The Holy Spirit is quenched when we fail to respond to Him and follow His direction either in our own lives or in a church service. When we resist or suppress the Holy Spirit, we are quenching Him. When we fail to reverence Him when He is dealing with people in a service, we are quenching Him. When people begin to get up and leave or start moving around during an altar call, this can be a big distraction that quenches the Holy Spirit.

"Ye stiffnecked and uncircumcised in heart and ears, ye do always resist the Holy Ghost: as your fathers [did], so [do] ye." (Acts 7:51)

This shows another reason that it is extremely important to get to know the Holy Spirit. He is the source of power not only in our own lives, but also in the life of the Church. Now let's look at the important part that the anointing played in the ministry of the Lord Jesus.

The Power Of The Holy Spirit In The Ministry Of Jesus

When Jesus came from heaven to earth, He was born of the

virgin Mary. He became the God man (the son of man as Jesus referred to Himself). Jesus did not perform any miracles before the Holy Spirit anointed Him. When He was about 30 years old, John baptized him in the Jordan River. "And the Holy Ghost descended in a bodily shape like a dove upon Him, and a voice came from heaven, which said, Thou art my beloved Son; in thee I am well pleased." (Luke 3:22)

Jesus began His ministry after the Holy Spirit's anointing came upon Him. So Jesus began His ministry with the power of the Holy Spirit. "How God anointed Jesus of Nazareth with the Holy Ghost and with power who went about doing good, and healing all that were oppressed of the devil; for God was with him." (Acts 10:38)

The School Of The Holy Spirit

The word tells us that immediately after Jesus became anointed with the Holy Spirit, the Holy Spirit led Him out into the wilderness. While Jesus was in the wilderness (a place of seclusion), He became familiar with and learned to be totally led by the Holy Spirit. I believe the Holy Spirit led Jesus to the "school of the Holy Spirit." I believe the Holy Spirit led Jesus to pray and fast for 40 days and during this time Jesus was being taught the ways of the Holy Spirit. The devil came to distract Him, to tempt Him, and to put doubt in His mind about His identity, His calling, His mission and His destiny.

Passing The Test

Jesus passed this test in His life. Jesus used the Word of God and the anointing as His defense when the attacks of the devil came. Because Jesus used the word, it kept Him from sinning and it put the devil on the run and Jesus came out of the wilderness full of the word and anointing of God. Jesus promised this same Holy Spirit would come to us. Jesus spoke about the Holy Spirit extensively in the book of John. Jesus prophesied that after He was crucified, raised from the dead, and ascended to heaven, He would send the Holy Spirit to come and take His place on the earth to live in us.

"In the last day, that great [day] of the feast, Jesus stood and cried, saying, if any man thirst, let him come unto me, and drink. He that believeth on me, as the scripture hath said, out of his belly shall flow rivers of living water. But this spake He of the Spirit, which they that believe on Him should receive: for the Holy Ghost was not yet [given]; because that Jesus was not yet glorified." (John 7:37-39)

Jesus talked about an event that was going to take place in the future. John the Baptist spoke of it when he was baptizing with water in Matthew 3:11. John said that he baptized with water but one was coming after him that would baptize with Holy Ghost Fire, so John was referring to Jesus who would later baptize believers with a different baptism. Jesus told the disciples that it was expedient that He should go away or the Holy Spirit would not come. "Nevertheless I tell you the truth; it is expedient for you that I go away: for if I go not away, the Comforter will not come unto you; but if I depart, I will send him unto you." (John 16:7)

We know that Jesus never did any signs and wonders without being anointed by the Holy Spirit. Jesus knew that we also would not be able to do any works for the Glory of God without the anointing of the Holy Spirit. Jesus was very adamant about us receiving the same power with which He was anointed. "Verily, verily, I say unto you, He that believeth on me, the works that I do shall he do also; and greater [works] than these shall he do; because I go unto my Father." (John 14:12)

"But ye shall receive power, after that the Holy Ghost is come upon you: and ye shall be witnesses unto me both in Jerusalem, and in all Judea, and in Samaria, and unto the uttermost part of the earth." (Acts 1:8)

When Did The Holy Spirit Come?

"And, being assembled together with [them], commanded them that they should not depart from Jerusalem, but wait for the promise of the Father, which, [saith he], ye have heard of me. For John truly baptized with water; but ye shall be baptized with the Holy Ghost not many days hence." (Acts 1:4-5) The Holy Spirit came on the day of Pentecost! "And when the day of Pentecost was fully come, they were all with one accord in one place. And suddenly there came a sound from heaven as of a rushing mighty wind, and it filled all the house where they were sitting. And there appeared unto them cloven tongues like as of fire, and it sat upon each of them. And they were all filled with the Holy Ghost, and began to speak with other tongues, as the Spirit gave them utterance. And there were dwelling at Jerusalem Jews, devout men, out of every nation under heaven. Now when this was noised abroad, the multitude came together, and were confounded, because that every man heard them speak in his own language. And they were all amazed and marvelled, saying one to another, Behold, are not all these which speak Galilaeans? And how hear we every man in our own tongue, wherein we were born? Parthians, and Medes, and Elamites, and the dwellers in Mesopotamia, and in Judea, and Cappadocia, in Pontus, and Asia, Phrygia, and Pamphylia, in Egypt, and in the parts of Libya about Cyrene, and strangers of Rome, Jews and proselytes, Cretes and Arabians, we do hear them speak in our tongues the wonderful works of God. And they were all amazed, and were in doubt, saying one to another, what meaneth this? Others mocking said, These men are full of new wine.

But Peter, standing up with the eleven, lifted up his voice, and said unto them, Ye men of Judea, and all [ye] that dwell at Jerusalem, be this known unto you, and hearken to my words: For these are not drunken, as ye suppose, seeing it is [but] the third hour of the day. But this is that which was spoken by the prophet Joel; And it shall come to pass in the last days, saith God, I will pour out of my Spirit upon all flesh: and your sons and your daughters shall prophesy, and your young men shall see visions, and your old men shall dream dreams: And on my servants and on my handmaidens I will pour out in those days of my Spirit; and they shall prophesy: And I will shew wonders in heaven above, and signs in the earth beneath; blood, and fire, and vapour of smoke: The sun shall be turned into darkness, and the moon into blood, before that great and notable day of the Lord come: And it shall come to pass, [that] whosoever shall call on the name of the Lord shall be saved." (Acts 2: 1-21)

We can see that once the Holy Spirit anoints us we are able to be effective witnesses for Jesus while we are on this earth. We must come into the revelation that we are anointed.

How To Know That You Are Anointed

When someone receives Jesus Christ as his Lord and Savior and becomes born again, that person becomes anointed. "Jesus answered and said unto him, Verily, verily, I say unto thee, except a man be born again, he cannot see the kingdom of God." (John 3:3)

Some people think that "Christ" is Jesus' last name. No, the word "Christ" in the Strong's Concordance is "Christos (khristos); anointed, that is, the Messiah, an epithet of Jesus: - Christ." "But the anointing which ye have received of him abideth in you, and ye need not that any man teach you: but as the same anointing teacheth you of all things, and is truth, and is no lie, and even as it hath taught you, ye shall abide in him." (1 John 2:27)

"Now he which stablisheth us with you in Christ, and hath anointed us, [is] God; who hath also sealed us, and given the earnest of the Spirit in our hearts." (2 Corinthians 1:21, 22)

As we learned earlier in this chapter, the anointing that we have comes from God and it separates us from the world and sets us apart as holy unto Him. Once a person receives Christ (the Anointed One) into his heart, he is immediately anointed.

The Anointing is not something that is achieved after reaching certain goals or levels of spiritual maturity, no the anointing comes by receiving Jesus as Lord.

A Well Anointing

The anointing that comes from salvation is what I call a **Well Anointing.** The anointing is not something that is achieved after reaching certain goals or levels of spiritual maturity. No, the anointing comes by receiving Jesus.

"Therefore with joy shall ye draw water out of the wells of salvation." (Isaiah 12:3) "But whosoever drinketh of the water that I shall give him shall never thirst; but the water that I shall give him shall be in him a well of water springing up into everlasting life." (John 4:14)

A person can teach and preach under this anointing and can operate in the gifts of the Holy Spirit. However, a person will be limited in two areas; One: their prayer life, and Two: the demonstration of Holy Ghost power.

A Deeper Anointing - The River Anointing

There is a deeper anointing that one can receive after salvation. "But God hath revealed them unto us by his Spirit: for the Spirit searcheth all things, yea, the deep things of God." (I Cor. 2:10) This deeper anointing that I'm talking about is what Jesus described in the seventh chapter of John.

This anointing comes from being baptized in the Holy Spirit. I call this a *River Anointing.* How does one experience the river anointing? "In the last day, that great [day] of the feast, Jesus stood and cried, saying, If any man thirst, let him come unto me, and drink. He that believeth on me, as the scripture hath said, out of his belly shall flow rivers of living water. But this spake He of the Spirit, which they that believe on Him - should receive: for the Holy Ghost was not yet [given]; because that Jesus was not yet glorified." (John 7:37-39)

I remember the first time I experienced the river anointing. I was seventeen years of age. I attended a Methodist high school in Tampa, Fl. I remember that during this time in my life I was seeking for more of God. I had read in the Bible about the gifts of the Holy Spirit and my pastor at the church I was attending was talking about being filled with the Holy

27

Spirit. In our school there was a required chapel service that all the students had to attend. During one of those chapel services, one of the teachers talked about the infilling of the Holy Spirit. At the end of His message he asked for all the students that would like to be filled with the Holy Spirit to come forward and the students that were already filled with the Holy Spirit to come and pray for those that had come forward.

Well, I was one of those that went forward to receive the infilling of the Holy Spirit. I remember that when I knelt down at the altar, one of the students asked me to repeat a prayer after him. He began by saying, "Lord Jesus, I thank you that I am born again, and you live in my heart. Lord Jesus, I need power in my life to be a better witness for you." I continued, "I want everything in the word of God that is for me. I ask you right now to infill me with your Holy Spirit." As soon as I finished the prayer, a stirring began deep on the inside of me; suddenly I began to pray out loud in an unknown language, very loudly. Ever since that day I have been experiencing the flow of that river anointing.

The Flood Or Floods

The Vine's Expository Dictionary defines a river as" a stream", "a flood or floods", or "the effects of the operation of the Holy Spirit in and through the believer." With the river anointing, your prayer life will be 100% enhanced! This is because the Holy Spirit in you with your spirit can pray out the mysteries of God. "For he that speaketh in an unknown tongue speaketh not unto men, but unto God: for no man understandeth him; howbeit in the spirit he speaketh mysteries." (I Corinthians 14:2)

"Likewise the Spirit also helpeth our infirmities: for we

28

know not what we should pray for as we ought: but the Spirit itself maketh intercession for us with groanings which cannot be uttered. And He that searcheth the hearts knoweth what is the mind of the Spirit, because He maketh intercession for the saints according to the will of God." (Romans 8:26, 27)

The Same Works As Jesus

With the river anointing, you will be a stronger witness for Jesus Christ because you will be anointed with Holy Ghost power to do the same works that Jesus did. "Verily, verily, I say unto you, he that believeth on me, the works that I do shall he do also; and greater works than these shall he do; because I go unto my Father." (John 14:12)

"And these signs shall follow them that believe: In my name shall they cast out devils; they shall speak with new tongues; they shall take up serpents; and if they drink any deadly thing, it shall not hurt them; they shall lay hands on the sick, and they shall recover." (Mark 16:17-18)

To more fully understand the river anointing, let us look at the doctrine of baptisms. In this next section we will be giving a number of scriptures to back up the point I am trying to get across, so please bear this in mind when reading.

The Doctrine of Baptisms

There are three baptisms a person can receive. First, we will lay a scriptural foundation. "Therefore leaving the principles of the doctrine of Christ, let us go on unto perfection; not laying again the foundation of repentance from dead works, and of faith toward God, Of the doctrine of baptisms, and of laying on of hands, and of resurrection of the dead, and of eternal judgment." (Hebrews 6:1, 2)

The word Baptism comes from three Greek words: Baptisma or Baptismos or Baptizo. In the Vine's Expository Dictionary these words have the following meanings:

1) Baptisma - Baptism: Consisting of the processes of immersion (to put in or under), submersion (to sink), and emergence (to rise or come forth, as out of water or anything that covers)

2) Baptismos - As distinct from Baptisma; this is used for the ritual of ceremonial washing of articles.

3) Baptizo - means to dip. Jesus commissioned His disciples to go into the entire world and teach and baptize. "Go ye therefore, and teach all nations, baptizing them in the name of the Father, and of the Son, and of the Holy Ghost." (Matthew 28:19)

The First Baptism A Person Can Receive Is:

1) A Baptism into Jesus

This is from salvation or becoming Born Again. We are baptized into the Body of Christ. "Jesus answered and said unto him, Verily, verily, I say unto thee, Except a man be born again, he cannot see the kingdom of God." (John 3:3)

"That if thou shalt confess with thy mouth the Lord Jesus, and shalt believe in thine heart that God hath raised him from the dead, thou shalt be saved. For with the heart man believeth unto righteousness; and with the mouth confession is made unto salvation." (Romans 10:9, 10)

"Behold, I stand at the door, and knock: if any man hear my voice, and open the door, I will come into him, and will sup with him, and he with me." (Revelation 3:20)

"Know ye not, that so many of us as were baptized into Jesus Christ were baptized into his death? Therefore we are buried with him by baptism into death: that like as Christ was raised up from the dead by the glory of the Father, even so we also should walk in newness of life." (Romans 6:3, 4)

"Therefore if any man be in Christ, he is a new creature: old things are passed away; behold, all things are become new." (2 Corinthians 5:17)

The Second Baptism A Person Can Receive Is:

2) The Baptism in Water

Baptism in water occurs when a person has received Jesus Christ as Lord and makes a public outward show of his conversion to Christ to demonstrate what Jesus has done inside him. The individual is immersed or submerged into water, symbolically burying the old self into a watery grave and then reemerging a new person in Christ (See Romans 6:3-4).

"And as they went on their way, they came unto a certain water: and the eunuch said, See, here is water; what doth hinder me to be baptized? And Philip said, If thou believest with all thine heart, thou mayest. And he answered and said, I believe that Jesus Christ is the Son of God. And he commanded the chariot to stand still: and they went down both into the water, both Philip and the eunuch; and he baptized him. And when they were come up out of the water, the Spirit of the Lord caught away Philip, that the eunuch saw him no more:

31

and he went on his way rejoicing." (Acts 8:36-39)

The Third Baptism A Person Can Receive Is:

3) The Baptism of Holy Ghost Fire

I know that I seem to be going on and on teaching and showing you how important it is for you to understand what types of baptisms there are. If there were not such controversy over these issues, then I could go on to something else. But I want to share a story here about the baptism of Holy Ghost Fire. Then I will go on teaching.

I was in the country of Panama back in the year 2001. One of my Spanish interpreters was named George and his wife's name was Mariela. George invited me and a pastor friend of mine who had come with me over to his home to have dinner. George spoke fluent English, but Mariela knew very little English. After dinner, George began to tell us that his wife had been desiring to be filled with the Holy Ghost fire. He told us that she had been seeking God for many days and had not yet been filled with the Holy Ghost or spoken in other tongues. So I told him that we would pray and lay our hands on her if she desired prayer.

After George spoke with her she agreed to have prayer. Through the translation from George to his wife, she repeated a simple prayer that I gave her to pray. As soon as she finished, my pastor friend and I laid our hands on her head. Suddenly she fell to the floor speaking in other tongues. Every time she tried to speak in Spanish, other tongues came out of her mouth. Later George told us that she was in that condition for three days. Every attempt to speak in Spanish only resulted in tongues. Now that is baptized!

John the Baptist said: "I indeed baptize you with water unto repentance: but he that cometh after me is mightier than I, whose shoes I am not worthy to bear: he shall baptize you with the Holy Ghost, and with fire." (Matthew 3:11) "And I knew him not: but he that sent me to baptize with water, the same said unto me, Upon whom thou shalt see the Spirit descending, and remaining on him, the same is he which baptizeth with the Holy Ghost." (John 1:33)

Jesus said that when you are baptized with the Holy Spirit you would have rivers of living water (the power of God) flow out of you. "In the last day, that great day of the feast, Jesus stood and cried, saying, if any man thirst, let him come unto me, and drink. He that believeth on me, as the scripture hath said, out of his belly shall flow rivers of living water. *But this spake he of the Spirit, which they that believe on him should receive, for the Holy Ghost was not yet given because that Jesus was not yet glorified.*" (John 7:37-39 italics mine)

"For John truly baptized with water; but ye shall be baptized with the Holy Ghost not many days hence." (Acts 1:5)

Receiving Power To Be A Witness

When you receive the Baptism of Holy Ghost Fire you will receive power to witness and be a vessel that God's healing power can flow through. "But ye shall receive power, after that the Holy Ghost is come upon you: and ye shall be witnesses unto me both in Jerusalem, and in all Judea, and in Samaria, and unto the uttermost part of the earth." (Acts 1:8)

When you receive the Baptism of Holy Ghost Fire, you will receive the evidence of that experience by speaking in different unknown languages.

"And when the day of Pentecost was fully come, they were all with one accord in one place. And suddenly there came a sound from heaven as of a rushing mighty wind, and it filled all the house where they were sitting. And there appeared unto them cloven tongues like as of fire, and it sat upon each of them. And they were all filled with the Holy Ghost, *and began to speak with other tongues*, as the Spirit gave them utterance." (Acts 2:1-4 italics mine)

"And these signs shall follow them that believe; In my name shall they cast out devils; they shall speak with *new tongues*; they shall take up serpents; and if they drink any deadly thing, it shall not hurt them; they shall lay hands on the sick, and they shall recover." (Mark 16:17, 18 italics mine)

"And it came to pass, that, while Apollos was at Corinth, Paul having passed through the upper coasts came to Ephesus: and finding certain disciples, He said unto them, Have ye received the Holy Ghost since ye believed? And they said unto him, We have not so much as heard whether there be any Holy Ghost. And he said unto them, Unto what then were ye baptized? And they said, Unto John's baptism. Then said Paul, John verily baptized with the baptism of repentance, saying unto the people, that they should believe on him which should come after him, that is, on Christ Jesus. When they heard this, they were baptized in the name of the Lord Jesus. And when Paul had laid his hands upon them, the Holy Ghost came on them; *and they spake with tongues*, and prophesied." (Acts 19:1-6 italics mine)

Is Baptism For Everyone? The Answer Is Yes!

"Then Peter said unto them, Repent, and be baptized every one of you in the name of Jesus Christ for the remission of

sins, and ye shall receive the gift of the Holy Ghost."
(Acts 2:38)

1) The word "repent" in the above verse refers to the initial repentance of a sinner unto salvation - *Baptism into Jesus.*

2) The phrase "baptized every one of you in the name of Jesus Christ for the remission of sins" refers to - *Water Baptism.*

3) The final phrase "and ye shall receive the gift of the Holy Ghost" refers to the - *Baptism of Holy Ghost Fire.*

How Can You Receive All Three Baptisms?

1) Ask Jesus to come into your heart and make Him the Lord of your life.

2) Find a local church and tell the minister that you have received Jesus as your Lord and Savior and that you want to be water baptized.

3) Now ask Jesus to baptize you with Holy Ghost Fire, then receive the Holy Ghost and begin to praise Him and thank Him. Then begin to speak in unknown tongues, not in your known language, but in the language that the Holy Spirit gives you. You will not understand this language, but God does.

"For he that speaketh in an unknown tongue speaketh not unto men, but unto God: for no man understandeth him; howbeit in the spirit he speaketh mysteries."
(1 Corinthians 14:2)

God's Power Through Us

Through us, God wants to demonstrate His power and glory before the world and the Church. For us to flow fully in the power of God, we need the river anointing, which comes only when we have been baptized in Holy Ghost Fire with the evidence of speaking in other tongues.

To summarize: A person becomes anointed when he receives Jesus as Savior. This is a well anointing. When someone is baptized in the Holy Spirit, he or she receives a river anointing. Fellowshipping and getting to know the Holy Spirit will help you in learning how to flow in the anointing. This will increase your ability to pray effectively, witness for Jesus, and demonstrate God's power - to heal, deliver, and set others free, to bring glory to God in heaven.

Chapter Three

How To Receive And Release The Anointing

M y wife Marie made a statement to me the other day.
She said,

"In your meetings you encourage people to drink from the
Holy Spirit or receive from the Holy Spirit."

She continued,

"Maybe people want to drink and maybe they want to
receive, but maybe they just don't know how."

I thought this could be true. People generally want to
receive a touch from God, but could it be that people may not
know how to receive from God?

Sometimes people can have a hard time receiving. Has any-
one ever come up to you and wanted to bless you with something and your response was *"Oh, you don't have to do that.
Really, it's O.K., you really don't have to do that."* People ask
God to bless them all the time. But when someone comes

along with a gift or wants to do something for them, they try really hard not to accept the blessing.

Learning To Be A Receiver

Learning to be a receiver is important when it comes to getting what we desire from God. First, let's go over some hindrances to receiving, then we will go over how to receive from God. *"What could be some obstacles that people have when it comes to receiving from the anointing?"* Here are a few:

I do not feel that I'm worthy

It is true, we are not worthy to receive from God. But the Word of God says that because Jesus took our sins and died on the cross for us, you and I become worthy to receive from God. It is God's grace that provides our worthiness. (see Ephesians 2: 8, 9)

Man made doctrine and religion

Religion and man made doctrine have stopped many people from receiving from the anointing. Some people believe that God is no longer doing miracles today. They believe that miracles ceased when the last apostle died. Some people are afraid of the supernatural. Any indication of a supernatural event is attributed to the devil.

Familiarity, Offense and Unbelief

These three things cause many people to fail to receive from the anointing. As we look in the word of God, we can see this. "And he went out from thence, and came into his own country; and his disciples follow him. And when the sabbath day was come, he began to teach in the synagogue: and many hearing [him] were astonished, saying, From whence hath this [man] these things? and what wisdom [is] this which is given unto him, that even such mighty works are wrought by his hands? 1. *Is not this the carpenter, the son of Mary*, the brother of James, and Joses, and of Juda, and Simon? and are not his sisters here with us? 2. *And they were offended at Him.* But Jesus said unto them, A prophet is not without honour, but in his own country, and among his own kin, and in his own house. And he could there do no mighty work, save that he laid his hands upon a few sick folk, and healed [them]. 3. *And He marvelled because of their unbelief.* And he went round about the villages, teaching." (Mark 6: 1-6 italics mine). We can see in this scripture that *familiarity, offense and unbelief* stopped the power of God even in the ministry of Jesus.

Receiving From The Anointing

Now that we understand some of the road blocks to receiving from the anointing, we can begin to learn the principles of receiving the anointing. We have to learn to yield to the things of God. This is not a formula, but some insight.

The Word says, "Neither yield ye your members as instruments of unrighteousness unto sin: but yield yourselves unto God, as those that are alive from the dead, and your members as instruments of righteousness unto God." (Romans 6:13)

But first you have to understand what yielding means.

The word "yield" in the Webster's Dictionary means "to allow; to concede; to surrender; to submit, to comply with; to give; to yield due praise; to permit; to grant; not to oppose; to give place; or to give up."

A better word to use when it comes to yielding to the Spirit of God is *surrender*, which means "to yield to the power of another; to give up; to resign in favor of another; to yield to any influence, passion or power." One of the Hebrew meanings for yield is *"being overcome."* Now that we understand what it means to yield ourselves, we must learn to surrender to the things of the Spirit.

How Does One Yield To The Anointing?

We yield to the Spirit by having an open heart to receive from Him whatever He desires to do in us and through us. We must allow God to work in us to do His great pleasure and purpose. That means that the Lord wants to change us, fill us, and work His work in us so that we can conform to the image of Jesus Christ on the outside of us. "For it is God which worketh in you both to will and to do of his good pleasure." (Philippians 2:13)

A few years ago I was at a meeting and the minister that was sharing had a very strong anointing in his life and ministry. After he was finished preaching he began to pray for people. There were not enough ushers to help catch the people who were being overcome by the power of the Holy Spirit so I decided to assist in catching people that were falling to the floor. I also wanted to be prayed for, but I wanted to serve first then receive prayer at the end. The time came that the minister asked for all that helped serve and wanted prayer to come up.

Pull On The Anointing

During the time he was praying for people he was doing some unusual things. With some people he would clap his hands over their heads or he would do a hand motion as if he was pulling something out of a person; it was a little different.

Many times when the power of God would come upon people they would scream or screech. Many of the people would fall to the floor shaking violently. Now it was my turn to receive prayer. Before I received prayer I said to the Lord, "If this is you, I'm going to drain this brother dry (referring to pulling on the anointing) but if this is not you just let this pass me right on by." I was about three feet from this preacher and as he made his way to me I felt the tangible presence of God. When he got to me he placed his hands right on my hands and I felt like the power of God was going right through me. I fell to the floor and started shaking uncontrollably. When I got up off the floor, God had imparted to me a fresh anointing.

Another example of surrendering to the Holy Spirit happened after I had just finished preaching a Sunday morning service. The power of the Holy Ghost was very strong and many were touched by God. The pastor's family and my family decided to meet up at a local restaurant to have some lunch. There were about eight of us together.

When we had arrived at the restaurant the server took us to our seats and said she would be back to take our orders. When she came back, all of us were talking about how powerfully God moved in the morning service and how excited we were about what God was going to do in the evening service.

As the server was taking orders she told the pastor's daughter that she too was converted the night before.

I overheard her telling her story so I asked her to tell me how she got converted.

41

She said, "I prayed to God to help me be a good person and to do right things."

I asked her why she did that.

She said her boyfriend was going to break up with her unless she went to church with him and read her Bible regularly.

I then said, "Pray this prayer with me."

She said "Ok!" and I led her in a simple salvation prayer and she received Jesus into her heart.

After she finished praying she looked up and said, "I'm different!"

Then suddenly she asked, "What is happening to me?"

"What do you mean?" I asked.

She said, "I don't know to cry or to laugh!"

So I went around the table and gently put my hand on her forehead and then she fell to the floor. Her life had been changed because she surrendered to Jesus and the Holy Spirit.

That night she came to the service and brought with her two other friends and they gave their hearts to the Lord and they too received a touch from God.

To Receive Or Not To Receive

I want you to notice that they had a choice to receive or not to receive, to surrender or not to surrender. You too have a choice as well; you do not have to receive what you don't want, whether it is from God or the devil. This is good to know.

You decide to whom you want to surrender.

I choose to surrender to everything God wants for my life, and you should too. In fact, this is what we must do; we must yield or surrender to God in worship; we must yield or surrender to God in our finances; we must yield or surrender to God our bodies; we must yield or surrender to God our families; we must yield or surrender to God in our hearts. "For ye are bought with a price: therefore glorify God in your body, and in your spirit, which are God's." (1 Corinthians 6:20)

How to Release The Anointing

When it comes to releasing the anointing there are some simple principles to apply. First we must understand that when it comes to operating in the realm of God it is all done by faith.

You may ask, "What is faith?"

The Webster's dictionary gives us several definitions pertaining to faith, among which is: "Belief; the assent of the mind to the truth of what is declared by another, resting on his authority and veracity, without other evidence; the judgment that what another states or testifies is the truth. I can have strong faith or no faith in the testimony of a witness, or in what a historian narrates."

My definition of faith is this: a firm belief in something

43

that is real before you see it, have it , or feel it. We cannot see God, but we know that He is real because you can see the evidence in the changed lives of people who have been saved, delivered, and healed and touched by the anointing.

Faith is simple belief.

Operating In Faith

The word of God tells us that without faith it is impossible to please God (see Hebrews 11:6). Anything and everything we do when it come to releasing the anointing is done by faith.

The anointing is released by faith and the anointing is received by faith.

Anytime a person comes to receive prayer or anytime a person prays for another person, it has to be done in faith.

Faith is the key to receiving from the anointing and faith is the key to releasing the anointing. We are responsible in releasing the anointing, but we are not responsible for the results. God is responsible for the results. It is He that gets all the praise and glory for the healings, signs and wonders.

Transference Of The Anointing

I want to take you to the greatest scripture that I have found in the word of God on the transference of the anointing. You may want to study this portion of scripture over and over. Get a picture in your mind's eye to what is really happening.

"And a certain woman, which had an issue of blood twelve years, and had suffered many things of many physicians, and had spent all that she had, and was nothing bettered, but rather grew worse, when she had heard of Jesus, came in the press behind, and touched his garment. For she said, "If I may touch but his clothes," I shall be whole. And straightway the fountain of her blood was dried up; and she felt in [her] body that she was healed of that plague. And Jesus, immediately knowing in himself that virtue had gone out of him, turned him about in the press, and said, "who touched my clothes?" And his disciples said unto him, thou seest the multitude thronging thee, and sayest thou, "who touched me?" and he looked round about to see her that had done this thing. But the woman fearing and trembling, knowing what was done in her, came and fell down before him, and told him all the truth. And he said unto her, "daughter, thy faith hath made thee whole; go in peace, and be whole of thy plague."
(Mark 5:25-34)

There are several key elements here in this portion of scripture pertaining to the transference of the anointing. We can see from this scripture that there was a woman that needed healing in her body. She went to all the doctors that she could. She spent all her money. She was sick for twelve years and was growing worse in her condition every day. The doctors could not do anything more for her. She was dying. This dear woman became desperate. The Word says "when she heard of Jesus." We know the Bible says in Romans 10:17 "Faith cometh by hearing and hearing by the word of God." I like to throw this in for free. *"And accepting as truth that which you hear."* People hear the Word all the time, but not everyone accepts it as truth.

Hearing Produces Activated Faith

Now I wonder what sort of things she might have been hearing about Jesus. I'm sure she was getting reports of all the healings and miracles Jesus was doing in the city and the regions round about. *This is the kind of reports people need to hear when they are ill.* Since she was hearing about all the good things Jesus was doing, faith began to rise up in her and she said, "If I could just touch His clothes, I shall be whole." Making this declaration of her faith and being willing to act upon what she believed caused healing power to be released into her. As you read the scripture, you see that as she touched Jesus' garment, virtue went out of Him. That virtue was the anointing that was released from Jesus and was received by the woman. When this woman placed a demand on the anointing and ministry of the Lord Jesus and acted on what she believed, she received her miracle.

The Purpose Of The Anointing

The purpose of the anointing is to destroy the works of the devil (see Isaiah 10:27 & I John 3:8b). The anointing sets people free.

I remember when I holding a meeting in Parsons, KS. A young lady came to the meeting with severe depression. When it came time for me to minister, I called several people out of the congregation and prayed for them. I was led to pray for this particular young lady. The power of the anointing hit her and she fell to the floor where she remained for two hours laughing uncontrollably under the power of the anointing. Later she wrote me her testimony telling me how she had been suffering from depression for some time. She stated in her letter that after she received prayer, she fell to the floor and started to laugh; when she got up off the floor, she was totally healed. Thank God for the name of Jesus and the power of the anointing.

The Anointing Within / The Anointing Upon

The anointing "within" comes from salvation and the river of the Holy Ghost that is present in you all the time. The anointing that comes "upon" us is for the purpose of serving. I always have the anointing that is "within" me, but when I am ministering to someone or operating in the office of the evangelist, the anointing "upon" me is working. The same applies to you in whatever God has called you to do.

Ways To Transfer The Anointing

The Word of God shows several ways that the anointing can be transferred; here are a few:

By the laying on of hands
Mark 16:18 "They shall take up serpents; and if they drink any deadly thing, it shall not hurt them; they shall lay hands on the sick, and they shall recover." "Therefore leaving the principles of the doctrine of Christ, let us go on unto perfection; not laying again the foundation of repentance from dead works, and of faith toward God, of the doctrine of baptisms, and of laying on of hands, and of resurrection of the dead, and of eternal judgment."(Hebrews 6:1, 2)

By the words of your mouth
Matthew 8:8 "The centurion answered and said, Lord, I am not worthy that thou shouldest come under my roof: but speak

the word only, and my servant shall be healed."

By the breath

John 20:22 "And when he had said this, he breathed on [them], and saith unto them, Receive ye the Holy Ghost."

A dead man's bones

2 Kings 13:20, 21 "And Elisha died, and they buried him. And the bands of the Moabites invaded the land at the coming in of the year. And it came to pass, as they were burying a man, that, behold, they spied a band [of men]; and they cast the man into the sepulcher of Elisha: and when the man was let down, and touched the bones of Elisha, he revived, and stood up on his feet." *Even after Elisha died, he still had the residue of the anointing in his bones.*

By anointed cloths

Acts 19:11, 12 "And God wrought special miracles by the hands of Paul, so that from his body were brought unto the sick handkerchiefs or aprons, and the diseases departed from them, and the evil spirits went out of them."

Clay and spit

John 9:6, 7 "When he had thus spoken, he spat on the ground, and made clay of the spittle, and he anointed the eyes of the blind man with the clay, and said unto him, Go, wash in the pool of Siloam, (which is by interpretation, Sent.) He went his way therefore, and washed, and came seeing."

There are other ways that the anointing can be transferred, but these are a few that you can study. Now that you understand some basic principles of the anointing, let's go on to find out ways to increase the anointing.

Chapter Four

How To Increase
The Anointing

There are several things we can apply to our lives to increase the anointing of God. In this chapter we are going to discover some of the aspects of increase. The *first thing* you can do to increase the anointing on your life is to *hunger and thirst* for more of God and seek Him with all your heart. Pursue God and cry out to Him. God promises us in Jeremiah 29:13, "And ye shall seek me, and find me, when ye shall search for me with all your heart." When you seek God, He will respond and you will receive a touch from Him. I received the touch of God in the second week of March 1993. Yes, I was born again at the age of twelve and filled with the Holy Spirit at the age of seventeen. But I experienced a touch of God that changed my life that night in 1993.

The Supernatural Touch Of A Mighty God

In 1993, God came and heard my cry. Marie and I had survived serious marital problems, and God had begun to restore our marriage. But we needed a restoration of joy and peace.

At the time, we had a janitorial business and were very busy day and night. I had an addiction that ruled my life and I was held captive by it. Listening to the radio, I heard there was going to be a revival meeting in Lakeland, Florida.

The Lord spoke to me in a very clear voice and said He wanted me to go to the meeting. He was going to do something for me. Marie and I went to the meeting. We sat close to the front of the church. When the minister began to preach, the people began to laugh uncontrollably.

Marie thought,

"How rude for people to be interrupting the service."

I was just listening to the message. Then the minister began praying for people. He called people out of their seats and they fell under the power of the Holy Spirit even though he didn't touch them.

Did You See That Holy Roller?

This really got my attention and a hunger rose up in me. As the minister made his way to the section of pews where we were sitting, the power of the Holy Spirit hit me, and I felt the power of God lift me up into the air, lay me on the floor and roll me toward the platform. I was helpless against the power that moved me to the front of the church. I was instantly delivered from the addiction, and all the hurts of my past. *I was totally set free!* "Like a mantle [thrown about one's self] You will roll them up, and they will be changed." (Hebrews 1:12a, AMP)

As I lay on the floor at the front of the church, I heard a clear, strong voice say,

"I have a work for you, and the greater the work I do in you, the greater the work I will do through you!"

On the way home from the church, I laughed uncontrollably, I could not stop. I told my wife Marie.

"I am changed!"

She replied,

"We will see how long this lasts!"

It has lasted, and today our joy is still very vibrant. I will never forget when I was set free: it was the second week of March 1993 on a Monday night in Lakeland, Florida at about 10:00 P.M. *God touched me and restored the joy of my salvation and delivered me of my past.* Once I came in contact with that anointing, I became familiar with that supernatural power, that supernatural anointing that comes from God. I want you to understand that the anointing is not a feeling but it can be felt. That day I felt God, instantly God became real to me. The anointing became real.

The *second thing you can do* to increase the anointing on your life is to *develop a lifestyle of prayer, fasting and study of the Word.* Prayer is not a ritualistic religious formula. No, prayer is a relationship with your heavenly Father. Prayer is communicating with God. There are all kinds of prayers that you can pray. Just remember that your prayer time is a communion time with God. The more time you spend praying, the more you will see your relationship with God developing. You become like those that you associate with. Study of the Word is important because it is God's love letter to us. It is one of the ways that God communicates with us. The Word of God tells us to pray without ceasing and to study the Word on a regular basis. Fasting denies your flesh and tunes your spirit into Gods. (see 1 Thessalonians 5:17 and 2 Timothy 2:15)

The *third thing* you can do to increase the anointing on your life is to remain *pure and holy*. "Who shall ascend into the hill of the LORD? or who shall stand in his holy place? He that hath clean hands, and a pure heart; who hath not lifted up his soul unto vanity, nor sworn deceitfully." (Psalm 24:3, 4)

In this ungodly world we live in, with all the things on t.v., commercials, internet, billboards and radio, how can one stay pure and holy in an unholy world? It really goes back to developing that relationship with God. Reading your Bible and staying in church is a big part of it. Be careful what you choose to see and hear and refuse to allow the devil to trap you in anything that will hurt your relationship with God. Remain humble and repentant. Out of your communion with God will come the increase of the anointing on your life.

Casting Your Shadow

Here is a good illustration in the natural world of your relationship to the son of God - Jesus. Any object that is in relation to the natural sun will cast a shadow. The farther an object is from the sun, the smaller the shadow that is cast. But if you take that same object and bring it closer to the sun, the object will cast a larger shadow. It is the same with your relationship with Jesus. The closer you get to Jesus, the anointing will cast a larger shadow from you. "Insomuch that they brought forth the sick into the streets, and laid [them] on beds and couches, that at least the shadow of Peter passing by might overshadow some of them." (Acts 5:15)

Another illustration in the natural would be an automobile reflector: just as the reflector reflects light, so you and I reflect Jesus. "Moreover the light of the moon shall be as the light of the sun, and the light of the sun shall be sevenfold, as the light of seven days, in the day the LORD bindeth up the breach of his people, and healeth the stroke of their wound." (Isaiah 30:26)

"And all of us have had that veil removed so that we can be mirrors that brightly reflect the glory of the Lord. And as the Spirit of the Lord works within us, we become more and more like him and reflect his glory even more." (2 Corinthians 3:18, NLT)

The *fourth thing* you can do to increase the anointing on your life is to *study the men and women of God* that have the anointing on them and are getting results for the kingdom of God. Paul said to follow him as he followed Christ. There are great men and women of God who are excellent examples to the Body of Christ. You can study godly men and women of old and those of today to find out how they have learned to increase the anointing in their own lives. A good example of this in the scriptures is the relationship that Elisha had with Elijah. "And it came to pass, when they were gone over, that Elijah said unto Elisha, Ask what I shall do for thee, before I be taken away from thee. And Elisha said, I pray thee, let a double portion of thy spirit be upon me." (2 Kings 2:9)

It would be a good idea to do an extensive study of the relationship that these two men had. I believe if you will apply the principles that we have covered so far, there will be a definite increase in the anointing in your life.

Picture Gallery

Revival meeting in Parsons, KS

The wind of the anointing touching kids

Revival meeting in Honduras

Altar call in Honduras

The anointing touches in Panama

Jorge and Mariela Moreno
Mariela is the lady that was filled with the Holy Spirit and for three days could only speak in tongues instead of her native language - Spanish.

Adults receive a touch of the anointing

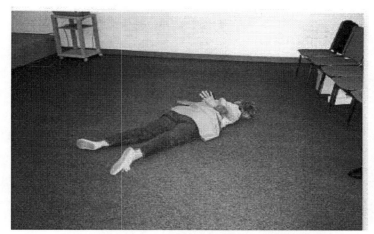

Woman delivered from demons

Young man healed from asthma

Woman healed from a severely injured leg

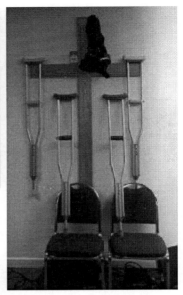

Woman healed from ovarian cyst. She is now married and has a brand new baby

The Joy of the Holy Spirit is manifested

Jack preaching in Mexico

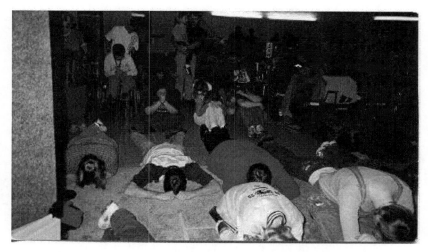

Teenagers repenting in a revival service

Chapter Five
Different Types Of Anointings

G od will never call you to do something without giving you the equipment to get it done. When Jesus began His ministry, He was fulfilling His destiny and calling. God gave Jesus the needed tools to accomplish this by anointing Him with the Holy Spirit. In the same way, for whatever God has for you to do while you are on this earth, there will be an anointing for you to be able to do it.

As we look into the Word of God, especially in 1 Corinthians chapters 12 through 14, we can see that there are many types of anointings and giftings. "All these [gifts, achievements, abilities] are inspired and brought to pass by one and the same [Holy] Spirit, Who apportions to each person individually [exactly] as He chooses." (1 Corinthians 12:11, AMP) Every one of us has the potential to flow in any of the gifts at any time as the Holy Spirit directs.

Although someone may be used in certain gifts consistently, it does not always follow that this is the ministry to which he or she is called. For example, every believer is to desire to prophesy; the simple gift of prophecy speaks to others to edify, exhort, and comfort (see 1 Corinthians 14:1-3). But every believer is not called to be a prophet. An example in the natural world would be that swimming in the water does not necessarily mean that you are a fish!

God does call many people to specific ministries. He has chosen some to be given as gifts to the body of Christ. In this chapter, we are going to discuss several different types of anointings for ministry. We will begin with the five fold ministry offices.

The Five Fold Ministry Gifts

The five "gifts" listed in Ephesians 4 are usually referred to as the five fold ministry gifts or offices. In each office, there are certain gifts or anointings that go with that particular office. "Wherefore he saith, when he ascended up on high, he led captivity captive, and gave gifts unto men. Now that he ascended, what is it but that he also descended first into the lower parts of the earth? He that descended is the same also that ascended up far above all heavens, that he might fill all things. *And he gave some, apostles; and some, prophets; and some, evangelists, and some, pastors and teachers; For the perfecting of the saints, for the work of the ministry, for the edifying of the body of Christ:* Till we all come in the unity of the faith, and of the knowledge of the Son of God, unto a perfect man, unto the measure of the stature of the fulness of Christ." (Ephesians 4:8-13, italics mine)

Notice that Jesus gave only some and not all. Only God can choose and anoint; man cannot. The Word says that many are called but few are chosen (see Matthew 22:14). Let me begin by saying that each office is unique in its function and no office is greater than any other. Each has a different role to play in the body of Christ.

The Apostle's office

First I would like to put to rest a misconception about the apostle's office before I discuss the role of this office. Some individuals would have you believe that the office of the apostle is the highest office and that they should rule over all the other offices. This is the verse that they like to quote to try to prove their point.

"And are built upon the foundation of the apostles and prophets, Jesus Christ himself being the chief corner[stone]; In whom all the building fitly framed together groweth unto an holy temple in the Lord." (Ephesians 2:20,21)

However, today the foundation is not still being established; it has already been built. It is true that the fulfillment of prophecy in the Old Testament brought about the New Testament. And it is true that the office of the apostle laid the foundation of the Gospel of Jesus Christ through the original twelve apostles. But today we are not still establishing the foundation of the the Gospel. We are already building upon that which has already been laid. We do this by advancing the kingdom of God through the conversion of the lost to salvation and by strengthening and perfecting the saints by the written word of God.

To understand the role of the apostle's office, you have to understand the meaning of the word "apostle". Strong's Concordance gives these definitions: "a delegate; specifically an ambassador of the Gospel; officially a commissioner of Christ ("apostle"), (with miraculous powers) - apostle, messenger, he that is sent."

Marks Of An Apostle

An apostle is simply a "sent-one". There are distinct gift-ings in this office that give proof to its authenticity. The marks of a true apostle are as follows. *One*: The person must be a teacher or preacher of the word of God. *Two*: The person will have outstanding spiritual gifts in operation in his or her min-istry. "Truly the signs of an apostle were wrought among you in all patience, in signs, and wonders, and mighty deeds." (2 Corinthians 12:12) When you study the ministries of those called apostles in the word of God, you will see outstanding gifts in operation: raising the dead, casting out devils, walking on water; also unusual manifestations of the Holy Spirit.

Third: The apostle will have had a deep personal experi-ence with the Lord. One example would be Paul who had a "road to Damascus experience." Another would be Peter, James, and John who had a "mount of transfiguration experi-ence". *Fourth*: The office of the apostle will have the ability to establish and organize churches in the places to which he has been sent. Some individuals today claim to be apostles and tell you that you have to submit to their authority and do what they tell you to do. But in the New Testament, the apostles only exercised this right over the works that they had estab-lished until the work could be overseen by a pastor. Because of the variety of things that the apostle must accomplish, there are many different gifts that will operate in this ministry office. The term missionary does not appear in the Bible but in all indication a missionary falls into the category of the apostle's office - only if the criteria is met.

The office of the Prophet
To stand in the prophet's office an individual must have

consistent manifestation of at least two of the three revelation gifts mentioned in in 1 Corinthians 12. The word of wisdom usually speaks of the future. The word of knowledge reveals things about the present or the past. The gift of discerning of spirits is the ability to see or hear into the spiritual realm; angels, demons, or even the Lord Himself may be seen. In addition, the things that the prophet has foretold should come to pass.

Three Types Of Visions

In the Old Testament, a prophet was known as a "seer". He or she was given the ability by God to "see" present or future events. God would communicate these things to the prophets through visions. There are three types of visions that a person can have.

The *first type of vision* is called a spiritual vision or a closed vision. These visions occur when your eyes are closed and you see into the realm of the spirit through your mind's eye. Dreams also fall into this category.

The *second kind of vision* is what we call an open vision. This occurs when you are totally awake and your eyes are open. God allows you to see into the spirit realm. "And he answered, Fear not: for they that [be] with us [are] more than they that [be] with them. And Elisha prayed, and said, LORD, I pray thee, open his eyes, that he may see. And the LORD opened the eyes of the young man; and he saw: and, behold, the mountain [was] full of horses and chariots of fire round about Elisha." (2 Kings 6:16,17)

The *third type of vision* is a trance; this is when you are totally alert, but your senses seem to be suspended and you

64

become unaware of the physical realm. You actually step over into the spiritual realm and see what is before you. This is what happened to Peter in the tenth chapter of Acts.

A prophet will have visions and revelations in his or her ministry. A true prophet will speak by divine inspiration only what God has revealed to him. He will operate in the manifestation of the gift of prophecy to a much greater degree than other believers. As one of the five fold ministry offices, there will also be a demonstration of other gifts of the Spirit in greater measure.

The office of the Evangelist

When I received Jesus as my savior at the age of twelve, I felt in my heart that I was called to the ministry. I did not answer that call until I was twenty-six and after I received a touch from heaven in 1993. After that, I answered the call to be an evangelist and I have been operating in that office for the past 10 years.

The evangelist is one who brings the message of good news. First and foremost, the evangelist is a preacher and proclaimer of the Word, although he or she may teach as well. Signs and wonders will follow this ministry - God gives this ministry supernatural advertisement. In particular, healings and miracles will occur. Three gifts of the Spirit that are in operation in this ministry are the word of knowledge, the working of miracles, and the gifts of healing. Because the supernatural is so evident in this office, it has the capacity to draw the lost as well as the saint.

The evangelist loves to win souls to Jesus; this gift helps the church to grow.

Evangelist Look A-Likes

There are many in the church today that claim to be evangelists, but according to the Biblical definition, they are not. Some say that they are "singing evangelists" or "poetic evangelists" or "drama evangelists"; these things can be a part of evangelism since we are all called to share the good news of the gospel with the world. Paul told Timothy to stir up the gift that was in him and "do the work of an evangelist" (2 Timothy 4:5) but Timothy was not an evangelist because he was a pastor. We must remember that a true evangelist will be a preacher of the word and have the supernatural in his or her ministry.

The office of the Pastor

There are probably more believers called to the office of pastor than any of the other five fold ministry gifts. The pastor is known as the under shepherd or overseer of the flock of God. The terms "elder" and "bishop" also refer to the pastor's office. A pastor can preach or teach, or both. One called to the ministry of a pastor will have a shepherd's heart; he or she will love the sheep, watch over them, and go through good and bad times with the ones that God has entrusted to him. This ministry calling is like a doctor who is a general practitioner - any of the spiritual gifts may operate according to the need of the sheep.

A Proper Example To The Body Of Christ

Pastors have governing abilities as well in order to properly structure the church. A pastor recognizes that he or she does not own the church, but is to lead and teach people in spiritual things and be a good example before them. They do not control, manipulate, or dictate to

66

God's people or those in other five fold ministry offices. A true pastor recognizes the other four ministry offices as assets to the church and co-labors with them to perfect the body of Christ. The other offices often seem to be traveling ministries while the pastoral office is more stationary and local. If a person in pastoral ministry does travel, it should be only on a very limited basis. Unless God is directing us, trying to step out of one ministry calling into another ministry office can be very detrimental to our ministry.

The office of the Teacher

Teaching can be a part of the other four ministry gifts, but the office of the teacher is a specific gift in itself. One called as a teacher does not teach out of natural ability, but by supernatural understanding received by revelation from the Holy Spirit. A teacher will be able to relay divine revelations in a way that can be clearly understood and gives practical instruction. Often the Word of God will be broken down and explained line upon line and precept upon precept.

The office of a teacher is instrumental in helping the body of Christ to grow up in spiritual things. It never brings the body of Christ down, but lifts it to higher revelations in the Word of God. A true teacher will operate in the gifts of the Spirit and will be able to cause others to hunger to know more of God and His Word.

A Variety Of Ministry Gifts

Now that we have a basic understanding of the five fold ministry gifts, I want to share a little about some of the diversity of gifts that are found in the church. "For as we have many members in one body, and all members have not the same office: So we, [being] many, are one body in Christ, and

every one members one of another. Having then gifts differing according to the grace that is given to us, whether prophecy, [let us prophesy] according to the proportion of faith; or ministry, [let us wait] on [our] ministering; or he that teacheth, on teaching; *Or he that exhorteth, on exhortation: he that giveth, [let him do it] with simplicity*; He that ruleth, with diligence; he that *sheweth mercy, with cheerfulness*."
(Romans 12:4-8, italics mine)

In this portion of scripture we can see several ministry gifts. Some of these may not be as spectacular in their operation as the five fold ministry gifts, but nonetheless their origin is still supernatural. I have italicized only three of them so that you can have just a glimpse of some of the other ministries that God can give to believers.

The first is the ministry of exhortation. This ministry encourages and uplifts the body of Christ. The ministry of exhortation is not a teaching or preaching ministry; it exhorts people to come to Jesus. In the past, some ministers of the gospel had exhorters who traveled with them. After the preaching of the Word, the exhorter would then get up and encourage people to respond to the altar call. My father-in-law, Mel Myer, is a wonderful exhorter. He lifts up and encourages people wherever he goes. Many people have told Marie and me what a tremendous mentor and blessing he is.

The second is the ministry of giving. This ministry is just as important as any other gift in the body of Christ. We should all be givers when it comes to supporting the gospel and live a lifestyle of giving. But God has anointed certain individuals with a gift to create wealth and distribute it as He chooses. It is important that those operating in this ministry gift not be prideful, haughty, or controlling. The third is the ministry of showing mercy. This refers not only to compassion and feeling sympathy for the hurts of others, but also to manifesting mercy by words or acts of kindness. Mercy is often part of benevolence ministries because it takes care of those who have been wounded or have need. (See Acts 6)

Deacons, Musicians, Intercessors, and Others

These three fall under the category of helps or service. Deacons are not a group of board members or business men that get together and tell the pastor of the church what he can and cannot preach or how he should and should not dress. Deacons are individuals who serve in the church. "And in those days, when the number of the disciples was multiplied, there arose a murmuring of the Grecians against the Hebrews, because their widows were neglected in the daily ministration. Then the twelve called the multitude of the disciples [unto them], and said, It is not reason that we should leave the word of God, and serve tables. Wherefore, brethren, look ye out among you seven men of honest report, full of the Holy Ghost and wisdom, whom we may appoint over this business. But we will give ourselves continually to prayer, and to the ministry of the word."(Acts 6:1-4)

Deacons as well as all in the church serve in the ministry to uphold the visions of the five fold ministry gifts that God has given them and they do this as unto the Lord. (see 1 Timothy 3:8-13 deacon requirements)

Team Players

Those who are a part of the worship team or prayer team also fall under the gift of helps. A worship leader can be gifted by God to be a psalmist. Worship leaders have the ability to lead others into the throne room of God during worship. An intercessor is a person who loves to pray. We should all pray for others, but an intercessor has an ability to persist in standing in the gap and bearing burdens for others, whether it be individuals, ministries, cities, or nations. In every opportunity to serve in the church, from the associate pastor to the janitor or nursery worker, there is an anointing that goes along with that specific area of service. God desires us to be faithful no matter what the task. (see Matthew 25:23)

Operating In Love

To summarize, God gives us the gifts and anointings that we need to accomplish His task for us here on this earth. 1 Corinthians 13 shows us that it is possible to operate in the gifts of the Spirit without love, but the results will be limited. We must remember that the gifts and callings of God are for the benefit of others and not to exalt ourselves or think more highly of ourselves than we should. As we choose to walk and minister in love, we will demonstrate the same flow of the anointing that was in our Lord Jesus Christ.

Chapter Six

Being Divinely Guided By God

As I was standing in a check out line at the local grocery store, I had my driver's license in my pocket. As I pulled out my check card to pay for the items I was purchasing, I didn't notice that my license had fallen out of my pocket to the floor. I left the store and went home. A few hours later, I needed my driver's license and when I looked in my wallet where I usually keep it, it was gone! Have you ever misplaced something very important and been unable to find it where it was supposed to be? Well, you guessed it - panic hit me.

O No! I Lost My License

I did what most people would do - I tried to retrace my steps and remember where I might have put it. All to no avail; I could not find my license. After calming down, I decided to ask the Lord where it could be. I was trying to be led of God in finding it. One thought came to mind, so I went and looked, but my license was not there. A second thought came to mind; I went and looked there, but my license was not there either. So I stopped and asked again, "Lord, where could my license be?" Then a third thought came to mind. "Call the grocery store: it is in the lost and found." I called the grocery store and talked to a clerk in the lost and found department who told me that my license was there and to come and pick it up. Thank God we can be led by Him!

When it comes to hearing and following God in the area of divine guidance, God wants and desires for his children to hear and follow Him. As you can see from my experience, sometimes this takes some practice. There are several ways in the Word of God to be led by His Spirit. In this chapter, you will discover how to be led and guided by God's Holy Spirit.

Laying The Foundation

First let us lay a foundation in being led by God. It is very important that we follow the guidelines in God's word as we are being led by His Spirit. The Word and the Spirit must agree. God will never lead you contrary to His word. There are many voices out there in the world today. "There are, it may be, so many kinds of voices in the world, and none of them [is] without signification." (1 Corinthians 14:10)

We must develop an ear for the voice of God. God is speaking today. The question is, "Have we developed a spiritual ear to hear Him when He speaks?" Jesus said in John 10:27, "My sheep hear my voice, and I know them, and they follow me." Jesus is our Great Shepherd. "Now the God of peace, that brought again from the dead our Lord Jesus, that great shepherd of the sheep, through the blood of the everlasting covenant." (Hebrews 13:20)

If Jesus is our Great Shepherd (and He certainly is), it would be a good idea to learn how to hear and obey when He guides and speaks to us. We start out learning this by pressing in to know His will for our lives.

Pressing Into God

"How do you press into God?"

"Ask, and it shall be given you; seek, and ye shall find; knock, and it shall be opened unto you: For every one that asketh receiveth; and he that seeketh findeth; and to him that knocketh it shall be opened. Or what man is there of you, whom if his son ask bread, will he give him a stone? Or if he ask a fish, will he give him a serpent? If ye then, being evil, know how to give good gifts unto your children, how much more shall your Father which is in heaven give goo things to them that ask him?" (Matthew 7: 7-11)

We press into God by seeking God with all our hearts. Psalm 91 describes it as finding a *secret place with God*. A place where you can go and be alone with God: this can be a place in your home, car, or office; a place where you and the Lord can talk. This is the place you worship Him. This is the place you have conversations with Him; where you talk to Him and He talks with you. This is a relationship between two. The relationship is not one sided with you doing all the asking and talking. No, the relationship you have with God is the kind of relationship between two best friends.

We must press into God to gain the fullness of the blessing of the Holy Spirit.

Following The Shepherd Jesus

"And I say unto you, Ask, and it shall be given you; seek, and ye shall find; knock, and it shall be opened unto you. For every one that asketh receiveth; and he that seeketh findeth; and to him that knocketh it shall be opened. If a son shall ask bread of any of you that is a father, will he give him a stone? or if [he ask] a fish, will he for a fish give him a serpent? Or if he shall ask an egg, will he offer him a scorpion? If ye then, being evil, know how to give good gifts unto your children: how much more shall[your] heavenly Father give the Holy Spirit to them that ask him?" (Luke 11:9-13)

God's word is the final authority when it comes to being led by God. God will never contradict His word. "And there are also many other things which Jesus did, the which, if they should be written every one, I suppose that even the world itself could not contain the books that should be written." (John 21:25) This pertains to the signs and wonders that Jesus performed while He was on earth, not what He said to us in His word. We should never get outside the Word that has been given to us when we are being led by the Lord.

God's true nature and plan comes through the Lord Jesus. Jesus said that He was the way, the truth, and the life. When we are led by God, we see that God's nature is in Jesus. "Jesus saith unto him, have I been so long time with you, and yet hast thou not known me, Philip? he that hath seen me hath seen the Father; and how sayest thou [then], Shew us the Father?" (John 14:9) To follow God is to look at Jesus. Many Christians say that they would do whatever the Lord told them to do, if they only knew what He wanted. We as Christians must develop our listening skills.

Positioning Yourself to Hear God's Voice

You position yourself to hear God's voice by developing a relationship with God. This is a daily walk with God. Just as you spend time with those who are close to you, so you must spend time with the Lord. "But they that wait upon the Lord shall renew [their] strength; they shall mount up with wings as eagles; they shall run, and not be weary; [and] they shall walk, and not faint. " (Isaiah 40:31)

Waiting on the Lord in prayer and worship helps develop this relationship. Treat God as though He is your best friend. Reading the Word on a daily basis also helps you to know God better. The closer you get to God, the more clearly you will hear His voice.

"Be not deceived; God is not mocked: for whatsoever a man soweth, that shall he also reap. For he that soweth to his flesh shall of the flesh reap corruption; but he that soweth to the Spirit shall of the Spirit reap life everlasting. And let us not be weary in well doing: for in due season we shall reap, if we faint not." (Galations 6:7)

Praying In The Spirit

Praying in the Holy Spirit tunes your spirit into the wave length of the Holy Spirit Who lives on the inside of you. "The spirit of man [is] the candle of the LORD, searching all the inward parts of the belly." (Proverbs 20:27) We must remember that God can speak to us in several ways, but the two main ways He speaks to us are through His Word and by the Holy Spirit within us to our spirits.

Man is made up of spirit, soul, and body. We must train our souls to listen to the voice of God. Our conscience plays a role with the voice of God. Our soul, mind, and conscience are the decision side of our nature. God will speak to us through these avenues. We will have a peace on the inside when making a decision for our lives. The decision may not make sense in the natural, but if we go with our heart or peace, we will be making the move that God wants for us. "And let the peace of God rule in your hearts." (Colossians 3:15a)

Ways God Guides Us

The Lord guides us in seven different ways.

1) The first way God guides us is through *His Word*. The Bible is God's love letter and instruction manual for us. This is the primary way to know the will of God for our lives. We must develop a working knowledge of God's Word, which is His perfect will, before we can develop any other way to hear from Him pertaining to His unknown will for our lives. God can speak to us through His Word in several ways. One way is that as we spend time in prayer with God, He can quicken (make alive) a scripture to our minds. He can also speak through our daily Bible reading; He can impress a scripture to our spirit - the Bible verse just seems to stand out.

2) The second way the Lord will guide us is through the *Inward Witness*. This can come as a *strong impression*; a knowing, a comfortable feeling, a peace, a perception or intuition. We must follow these promptings (Proverbs 20:27). We must remember that the Holy Ghost is on the inside of us. The closer we get to Him, learning to know Him and His voice, and as we become more sensitive to Him, the more clearly we will understand and respond to Him no matter what the circumstance we are in.

3) The third way the Lord will guide us is through the *Inward Voice of Your Spirit*. This is the *still small voice*. "And after the earthquake a fire; [but] the LORD [was] not in the fire; and after the fire a still small voice." (1 Kings 19:12) This is also the voice of your conscience. Your conscience and

the Holy Spirit will bear witness with each other (see Romans 9:1). Never override your conscience because your conscience and the Holy Spirit have a relationship. When you are doing something, or about to do something that is contrary to the Lord's commands, there will come conviction - not condemnation. We are convicted so that we will repent and be cleansed.

Condemnation is caused from guilt - after repentance.

4) The fourth way God guides us is through *The Voice of the Holy Spirit - The Voice of Authority.* This can come one of two ways. One: a loud inaudible voice inside of you. In Acts 10:19, Peter was in a trance and heard the voice of the Holy Spirit speaking to him. Two: an audible voice - it is audible to your ears. In John 12:28-29, Jesus was speaking to a group of people. When He asked the Father to glorify His name, suddenly there was a voice came from heaven; some thought that it had thundered, but Jesus said that the Father had spoken. We are not to seek to hear voices. If God wants to speak to us audibly, He can, but it is better to hear the inward witness.

Most of the time I am led by God four ways. One: the Word of God. Two: the inward witness. Three: the still small voice. Four: the voice of authority. The loud voice of authority has happened only a few times in my life. This voice is loud and strong and very direct. There was only one time that I heard the voice of God audibly and that was when the touch of God fell on me in 1993.

5) The fifth way God guides us is through *Spectacular Guidance through Prophecy.* We must judge prophecy and it must bear witness with what God has already told us. Prophecy is confirmation, not information unless there is a word of wisdom which pertains to your future or some future

event. In the case of information, you should judge it; if it is not confirming what God has said to you, then put it on the shelf. By no means are we to go ahead and do things based on a prophecy that is only information: you may end up out of the will of God.

6) The sixth way God guides us is through *Visions*. This can happen in one of two ways. One: through closed visions. While your eyes are closed, you can see into the spirit realm in your mind's eye. Dreams are also in the category of closed visions. We see that Joseph was led by God in dreams to protect the baby Jesus from Herod. Two: through open visions. While your eyes are open and your senses are intact, you may see the Lord Himself, angels or demons - the gift of discerning of spirits is in operation. This is seen very strongly in the prophet's office. The Holy Spirit will show you things that are present or things to come.

My Experience With Visions

Many times what is seen in visions will show us things that will come or a course of action to take. Sometimes visions are for the purpose of increasing our understanding of spiritual truths that apply to our lives or situations.

I have only had a few visions in my life. The first one I had happened when I was the head maintenance man for a mall in Florida. One night some older teenagers were creating problems for some of the store clerks. One of them, with four of his friends, decided to pick a fight with me. The police were called and a report was filed. That night when I got off work and was on my way out to my car, I noticed that one of my car windows was knocked out. When I saw this, I was gripped by the fear of being alone at night in this big mall. I had to go to work the next night. After I arrived at work, before clocking in, I went up into the storage area and got on my knees and prayed,"Lord, please protect me tonight." As my eyes were closed, suddenly I could see four big angels dressed for battle, one on each side of the building. My fear was immediately gone and did not return.

The second closed vision that I experienced was shortly after God touched my life in 1993. I was in a revival service in Lakeland, Florida. During the time of worship, I had my eyes closed. Then suddenly I found myself up above the world in space looking down at the earth; everything was in color. I could see thousands of people from every continent and nation bowing down and worshipping God. As I looked over the horizon, I saw a wooden cross come up over it which was planted on the top of the world. Then suddenly it caught on fire and burned to ash. Then a second cross came up over the horizon, but this one was glowing with a powerful light. As I looked up, a great white sheet came out of heaven and covered the brightly glowing cross and the whole earth. I asked the Lord what this vision meant.

He said,

"The wooden cross was a cross that all the sins of the world fell upon, and my fire consumed them forever. The glorious bright cross was a cross of total victory for the world through what I accomplished on the cross. The great white sheet is symbolic of my Holy Spirit that covers the entire earth and draws all people to me as I am lifted up."

It was an awesome experience with God.

Sometimes God has shown me future events for my life

and ministry. I remember one dream that I had even before I was in the ministry. One afternoon, as I was napping, I fell into a deep sleep. Suddenly I found myself on a stage preaching to hundreds of people. I called for people to come and get saved. Hundreds of people came to the altar. After leading them in a prayer of salvation, I went to the right side of the platform and told the people to lift their hands. I waved my hand and said,"Be blessed in Jesus' name!" Then hundreds of people fell under the power of the Holy Ghost. Then I awoke praising God. This dream has come to pass. Now I can testify that after ten years in ministry that I have seen thousands come to know Jesus as Savior and have seen hundreds fall under the power of the Holy Ghost.

7) The seventh way God guides us is through a *Trance.* Your eyes may be opened or closed, but your physical senses are suspended. The veil of heavenly things is removed. During a church service, while standing behind the pulpit, Maria Woodworth Etter fell into a trance that lasted three days. It was reported that people fell under the power of God within a hundred mile radius. At the end of the trance, she picked up right where she had left off in her sermon.

Overview

God guides us in many different ways. We need to become more sensitive to the ways He does this. God is a diverse God. He desires to talk with us and lead us. As we seek Him in all we do, God will always lead us. At times, we may not like to go where He leads, but being in the perfect will of God is where the blessing will be. As we follow where He leads, we will find ourselves flowing in the anointing. This is our Shepherd, Jesus. "The LORD is my shepherd; I shall not want. He maketh me to lie down in green pastures; he leadeth me beside the still waters. He restoreth my soul: he leadeth me in the paths of righteousness for his name's sake. Yea, though I walk through the valley of the shadow of death, I will fear no evil: for thou [art] with me; thy rod and thy staff they comfort me. Thou preparest a table before me in the presence of mine enemies: thou anointest my head with oil; my cup runneth over. Surely goodness and mercy shall follow me all the days of my life: and I will dwell in the house of the LORD for ever." (Psalm 23)

Chapter Seven
Knowing Your God Given Authority

Because of what Jesus did on the cross, God has given us authority over many things on this earth. In this chapter, we are going to discuss how our authority pertains to our flowing in the anointing. For a more complete study of our total authority as believers, I highly recommend the Rev. Kenneth E. Hagin's book, "The Authority of the Believer."

To better understand our authority, we have to look back to the beginning in the book of Genesis. This is where we will discover what God's original intention was for mankind. "So God created man in his [own] image, in the image of God created he him; male and female created he them. And God blessed them, and God said unto them, Be fruitful, and multiply, and replenish the earth, and subdue it: and have dominion over the fish of the sea, and over the fowl of the air, and over every living thing that moveth upon the earth." (Genesis 1:27,28 italics mine)

Lost Authority

We can see from this scripture that God gave to Adam and Eve authority on this earth. God told Adam and Eve to subdue

the earth and to have dominion over it: man was set in charge of the earth. When satan deceived Eve, the authority that belonged to Adam and Eve was turned over to him and satan became the prince of this world.
(see John 14:20 and Matthew 4:8,9)

Because of sin, Adam and Eve were driven out of the Garden of Eden; the authority that had been given to them was lost. From that moment, a curse was placed on the earth by satan: man now had to work by the sweat of his brow and the woman would have pain in childbirth. Sickness and disease, poverty and lack and every evil work became present in society. Once man had the knowledge of good and evil, satan had control and dominion of the earth.

What satan Stole / Jesus Restored

When Jesus left heaven and came to earth, He was on a mission to destroy the works of the devil (see 1 John 3:8b). Jesus accomplished this by leaving heaven and being born of the virgin Mary. He was anointed by the Holy Spirit as He was baptized in the Jordan River; He went about doing good and healing all who were oppressed of the devil; He died on the cross, went down into hell, took the keys of death, hell, and the grave from satan, then preached to the ones in paradise; He rose from the dead, ascended in bodily form up to heaven, and sprinkled His Blood on the mercy seat, thus sealing our redemption and giving us back our dominion on the earth.

Because of what Jesus did, we once again have authority on this earth over the power of the devil. We have authority over sickness and disease, poverty and lack, and every evil work not only in our own lives, but in those of our families. "Then he called his twelve disciples together, and gave them power and authority over all devils, and to cure diseases. And he sent them to preach the kingdom of God, and to heal the sick." (Luke 9:1,2)

We do not have authority over people, but we do have authority over any demonic presence that negatively influences them. "Behold, I give unto you power [or authority] to tread on serpents and scorpions, and over all the power of the enemy: and nothing shall by any means hurt you." (Luke 10:19, paraphrase mine)

A person that has demons or demonic oppression and wants to be free can be delivered: this is done by the power of the anointing and the name of Jesus.

Jesus Walked In Total Authority

After Jesus became anointed He stepped into the fullness of what He was called to do.

That included authority!

When He would teach or preach, His authority was very evident. "And they were astonished at his doctrine: for he taught them as one that had authority, and not as the scribes." (Mark 1:22) If you read the first chapter of Mark, you will see Jesus walking in total authority. If Jesus walked in total authority, then you and I can walk in total authority.

Jesus is our example!

From the Word of God, let me give you an overview of events that show the authority that Jesus walked in while He was on this earth. Jesus healed the sick, raised the dead, calmed storms, walked on water, cast out demons, paid taxes with money from the mouth of a fish, multiplied food to feed thousands of people on two different occasions. He was transfigured in front of Peter, James, and John. He was raised from the dead and rose up into heaven before a group of people.

Jesus has delegated the same authority that He walked in to us. "And Jesus came and spake unto them, saying, *All power [authority] is given unto me in heaven and in earth.* Go ye therefore, and teach all nations, baptizing them in the name of the Father, and of the Son, and of the Holy Ghost: Teaching them to observe all things whatsoever I have commanded you: and lo, I am with you always, even unto the end of the world." (Matthew 28:18-20, paraphrase and italics mine)

All we have to do is believe it!

Jesus gave back to the church, His body, that which was lost during the time Adam and Eve were on earth. Jesus was the "second Adam" and he totally restored what the first Adam had lost. "And so it is written, the first man Adam was made a living soul; the last Adam [was made] a quickening spirit." (1 Corinthians 15:45)

Jesus The Restorer

You may say,"But Jack, if Jesus restored everything Adam lost, then why is the world in the state it is in?" If you will read the previous verse again, you will see that it says that Jesus was made a quickening spirit. That means that we have authority spiritually; in turn, it will affect everything naturally. Jesus said, "And I will give unto thee the keys of the kingdom of heaven: and whatsoever thou shalt bind on earth shall be bound in heaven: and whatsoever thou shalt loose on earth shall be loosed in heaven." (Matthew 16:19) We are still living under the curse of the fall, but we are not still living under the curse of the law. In Jesus, we have spiritual authority - we must discover what our rights are and begin to exercise those legal rights to enable us to flow in the anointing.

Conclusion
Final Words

We pray that this book has ministered to you. It is our desire for you to experience the anointing in your own life, every day. Remember, the anointing is available to you. It is not just here today, gone tomorrow.

We should never let the things we receive from God slip in our lives, but we should ever be growing in God. (see Hebrews 2:1)

The enemy knows that if he can stop the anointing in the lives of believers, he can stop the body of Christ from fulfilling its destiny. If he can keep the church in an ignorant state concerning the anointing, he wins, because the church will not be operating in the power Jesus gave us to defeat him.

Understand the time in which we are living. These are the last days. You were born for such a time as this. Time is coming to a close for this age. The anointing is necessary for all believers. It is the only thing that separates Christianity from all other religions in the world. We have the power of God to back up what we preach.

Go forth and flow in the anointing that the name of the Lord Jesus Christ will be magnified in all the earth!

About The Author

Rev. Jack Myers was born again at the age of twelve and filled with the Holy Spirit at the age of seventeen. He went to Christian school all of his life. At nineteen, he married his lovely wife and they have two wonderful boys.

Jack sensed the call of God at a very young age. In March of 1993, at the age of twenty-six he answered that call to the ministry after attending a revival meeting and having an encounter with the Holy Spirit unlike any he had ever had before. Later in 1995 Jack and his family moved to Broken Arrow, Oklahoma to attend Bible school.

Jack and his wife Marie graduated Rhema Bible Training Center in 1997. Rev. Myers is currently in the process of getting his Master of Divinity degree through correspondence at Life Christian University in Tampa, Florida.

He is a licensed and ordained minister with Rhema Ministerial Association International (RMAI) and is also an active member of International Convention of Faith Ministries (ICFM). He and his family are members of Rhema Bible Church in Broken Arrow, Oklahoma.

Jack has been in the traveling ministry since 1995, and he conducts revivals and open air crusades in the U.S and overseas. Jack preaches strong messages on holiness, repentance, joy, and revival. He also has a strong emphasis on the Holy Spirit and His working. God is a God of the heart, and if the heart is the root of the problem, that is where God can do His greatest work.

The revivals are similar to the revivals of the past, in that God confirms the Word preached with signs and wonders following. Many miracles and healings take place in the services, not only in the physical body, but also in the mending of broken hearts. There are also many rededications, salvations, water baptisms, and baptisms of the Holy Spirit. Many times the Holy Spirit moves on the ones that respond to the altar call, and they begin to weep in brokenness or receive joy in the Holy Ghost from God.

For additional copies of this book or a complete list of Jack's other tapes and materials, or to contact the ministry for speaking engagements please visit the web address below:

Jack Myers Ministries
"World Revival Evangelistic Association, Inc."

http://www.JackMyersMinistries.com

Jack Myers Ministries is a nonprofit, tax-exempt Bible preaching ministry and is available to minister as the Lord directs in any Church denomination, prayer meeting, prison, school, etc., on a love-offering basis.